TENTMAKERS SPEAK

Practical Advice from Over 400 Missionary Tentmakers

By Don Hamilton

**GL
Regal Books**
A Division of GL Publications
Ventura, California, U.S.A.

Published by Regal Books
A Division of GL Publications
Ventura, California 93006
Printed in U.S.A.

Scripture quotations in this book are taken from the HOLY BIBLE, NEW
INTERNATIONAL VERSION. Copyright © 1973, 1978, 1984 International
Bible Society. Used by permission of Zondervan Bible Publishers.

Library of Congress Cataloging-in-Publication Date (applied for).
ISBN 0-8307-1321-2

Tentmakers Speak

This book is dedicated to Dr. J. Christy Wilson Jr., the tentmaker *par excellence*, whose godly life has greatly influenced my own, and who, with his wife Betty, has always encouraged me.

Tentmakers Speak

ACKNOWLEDGEMENTS

Tentmakers Speak

This book could not have been written without the input from the tentmakers who responded to a survey conducted in 1985 and 1986. Many of them are anonymous, and the remainder are not mentioned by name. They are the real authors of this book.

Dick Staub and the team at Tentmakers International have been most supportive in this research.

Monnie Brewer of Grace Community Church and Bob Provost of Master's College have provided great incentive in pursuing the writing of this book even while delaying agreed-on programs for them.

The members of the former Board of Directors of Overseas Counseling Service, Cleo Shook, John Kyle, David Howard, Greg Livingstone and Monnie Brewer, have given great inspiration to plow through the thousands of comments received from the tentmakers and organize them for writing this book.

Special acknowledgement is given to Dr. Dean Kliewer of Link-Care for a substantial part in the editing and organizing of the book, and for unstinting personal encouragement and help for me.

Particular thanks is extended to John Holzmann

who undertook a major rewrite of the book.

The continual, warm, supportive role of my wife of 40 years, Charlotte, is also humbly and gratefully acknowledged. I praise God for such a help-mate!

Tentmakers Speak

Grace Community Church and Master's College and Seminary have long believed in the centrality of the church in world missions, and in the responsible involvement of lay-people in this task.

From the *Hamilton Tentmaker Survey Research Report #1*, we were convinced that here at last was the embryo of a truly practical means of preparing effective tentmakers for service overseas.

We are working with Don, both in the preparation of a tentmaker training curriculum at Master's, and also in the development of an evaluation and training tool for the church. Both of these programs will be made available to colleges, seminaries, and other churches. We share Don's convictions and enthusiasm about tentmaking.

Paul was a tentmaker, not because there was no other option, but because it was the best option to reach many segments of society. He wanted to be an example of how a Christian lives in this world. He wanted to earn the right to be heard based on his lifestyle, the careful building of relationships, being where the people were, working side-by-side with them. That's what we want for our people today.

Whether or not you end up overseas as a tentmaker, the kind of dedication, ministry experience, and relationship to the Lord discussed here will better prepare you for whatever ministry God has for you.
John MacArthur
Panorama City, CA
October 1987

My initial two-year tentmaking experience was life-changing. It was difficult to come home and be expected to be as I had been. I couldn't be the same: my priorities were different; my compassion for people was greater; and the materialism of America was suddenly rather offensive.

— Linda

Will the Good Tentmakers Please Stand Up?

For four years I worked with Overseas Counseling Service (now two organizations: Tentmakers International and Global Opportunities). I had the privilege not only of counseling prospective tentmakers, but of observing what was happening with tentmakers already overseas. It didn't take a lot of skill to realize that some tentmakers were better fruit-bearers than others. The question was, what made the difference? What set some apart from their peers? There are over a million American evangelicals overseas at any one time; why aren't they producing fruit like some?

I had some good ideas. I knew that many Christians—even evangelicals—have no interest in evangelizing the people around them. But what about those who do? What about those who go overseas with the specific idea in mind that they are going to make disciples?

This book is an outgrowth of a study on tentmakers I conducted in 1985 and 1986. With the help of several experts in the areas of tentmaking and psychological and statistical analysis, I designed a questionnaire to measure factors that contribute to tentmakers' effectiveness as witnesses for Christ. The questionnaire included 131 true-false or multiple-choice questions and two open-ended questions:

1. What else would you like to share about your tentmaking experience?

2. What advice would you have for those preparing to go as tentmakers in the areas of:

a. Biblical and spiritual preparation?

b. Secular and ministry experience?

c. Relationships and support on the field?

Over 800 tentmakers were sent the questionnaire; 406 responded. Of the 406 who responded, 98 percent answered the last two questions as well. Most of them filled the space allotted, and many attached additional sheets—286 additional pages in all.

In 1986, *Report #1* was issued. The Appendix is a summary of that report. When we released *Report #1*, we knew we needed to write a separate report based on the wealth of information contained in the thousands of comments to the open-ended questions.

The bulk of the material in this book comes from those responses. For security's sake and anonymity, I've changed people's names and identities. I've also edited their comments for readability, and, again for readability, occasionally merged several people's comments into one. *But the comments in this book attributed to tentmakers are the statements of tentmakers*; they come from real, live people who've "been there" on the field. They know what it's like. The wisdom here is not the "wisdom" of armchair experts' expectations or conjectures. It is the wisdom of experience.

The purpose of this book is practical. It is to help people interested in becoming tentmakers, first of all to understand what is involved in successful tentmaking; and second, to motivate them to do what is necessary to adequately prepare themselves for a successful ministry. Comments like the following were frequent:

I thought I was well prepared with 6 years of college ministry participation under my belt before going. Not so! I don't consider myself as having been a very effective minister of Christ on the field, because of a lack of preparation, a lack of fellowship, and a lack of accountability.
    —Jerry, a tentmaker in China

The opportunity to be a tentmaker came so suddenly, I made no specific preparations. I know now that *I should have been preparing ahead of time.*
    —Sarah, a tentmaker in the Middle East

I could have used much more preparation.
    —John, a tentmaker in Japan

A person going overseas as a tentmaker should not count on having the time to remedy deficiencies after getting to the field. *They should do their preparation before leaving the U.S.*
    —Harold, a tentmaker in North Africa

I don't believe anyone seriously considering a tentmaker ministry can afford to close his ears to what those who are out there are saying.

On the other hand, everything said by these tentmakers cannot be considered valid in every circumstance. Many went overseas before mission agencies took the tentmaking option seriously. It is significant that nearly 30% of the respondees were with mission agencies. Many others tried to affiliate with mission agencies and had been rebuffed, and reported on their disappointment. The comments could have been edited to temper some of the negative responses, but then it would not have authenticly reflected the thinking of these 406 tentmakers.

A subsequent book will explore a comprehensive, balanced viewpoint, taking into account the contents of this book, and bringing the concept of tentmaking up-to-date, including options which most of the tentmakers of this book did not have.

It's exciting to be on the cutting edge of what God is doing in the world today, and certainly tentmaking is one of God's strategies today.

Don Hamilton
Duarte, California
October 1987

I met some rather pathetic examples of Christians while overseas. Some of these fell into sin, lacked guidance and drew away from responsibility. I attribute their problems to lack of proper support or people to be accountable to.

— Greg —

CHAPTER ONE

So You Want to be a Tentmaker?

S uppose your pastor were to stand up and say, "Today we want to pray for Ron and Sue Lambeth, our missionaries in Caracas, Venezuela."

The heads of many people in the congregation snap back, and several turn to each other with questioning looks on their faces. You overhear several comments:

"What?!! Missionaries?!? Lambeths?!?"

"Did he say *Lambeths*?"

"Isn't Ron with Shell Oil? He makes over $100,000 a year!"

"What's Pastor doing saying the Lambeths are our *missionaries*?"

Well, Ron and Sue Lambeth really exist (though those aren't their names). They went to Venezuela and started an evangelistic Bible study on Tuesday nights. Ron invited his colleagues in industry and government to come. The study met with such success that soon they had to start an additional study on Thursday nights. Both studies grew until another was begun on Saturday nights. Soon the Tuesday night group became a house church.

Yes, Ron and Sue Lambeth planted a church

while "serving" an oil company in Venezuela.

Tentmaker to the Chinese

A few years ago, Joe Latimer and five other students from his college went to China on an exchange program. Joe had a degree in physical science, so while he studied Mandarin, he was also assigned to teach at a college of physical culture on the outskirts of Beijing.

Things began smoothly enough for the six Americans, but it wasn't long before some of them were winging their way back to the United States. The rigors of living in China were too much to handle. One was unwilling to tolerate the restrictions on his personal freedom. One was sent home on allegations of immorality, and a couple of others were expelled for unruly behavior. By the middle of the year, Joe was the only American left.

It was about this time that three Chinese students approached him to find out what made him so different.

"You're not like the others," they said. "Why is that?"

To Joe, it was a perfect opening for his Christian testimony. He was tempted to stop what he was doing right then and take the time to answer their question. But, being committed to maintaining high standards both on and off the job, and knowing there would be greater freedom of conversation in another setting, he invited them to come to his room in the dorm that night. They agreed, and he went on with his work, secure in the knowledge that if the Holy Spirit was truly leading them, the three young men would be there at the dorm.

Sure enough, that night, not only did the three show up, but several other students came by to find out what made Joe tick.

"So," they said as he poured them tea. "Why are you different?"

"Well," he responded, "it has to do with Jesus . . . ."

Over the course of several weeks, Joe led three of those students to faith in Christ, and he began discipling them. These younger brothers in the Lord showed every sign of new life in Christ.

At the end of the school year, Joe's contract was up. He had to leave China. He was extremely concerned. What would become of his disciples? Would the government let him return? He figured there was little hope of that. His extra-curricular activities hadn't gone completely unnoticed.

No sooner did he get back to America, however, than a letter came asking him to return for the next school year. Apparently, the authorities felt his integrity and his quality of work made his Christian influence worth the risk.

When Joe got off the plane that fall, Chao, one of the three men whom he had discipled, was waiting at the airport. He had an ear-to-ear grin on his face and two friends for Joe to meet. One of the two was a Christian whom Chao had led to the Lord while Joe was gone.

Later that evening, when they were alone, Chao asked Joe, "Do you have materials? I want to teach Deng."

Chao was only half a step ahead of his disciple—and knew he was in desperate need of training. Joe couldn't have been happier.

5

During Joe's second year, school administrators asked him to teach a course on American holidays. A group of 60 Chinese exchange students were going to America, and their professors thought they should know something about American culture.

"There's no way I can talk about American holidays without discussing Christianity," Joe said. "I can't explain Christmas, Easter, or Thanksgiving without mentioning Jesus or God."

"That's all right," the administrators said. "Whatever it takes."

When the class began, there were not only the 60 students who planned to go to America. With them were another 60 interested people, including some of the university staff! Joe still lives in China. He married a Chinese Christian girl, and hopes to spend the rest of his life there. Most recently, he has been asked to help set up a program to recruit additional teachers of English for China. And the authorities who asked him said, "Be sure you get people just like you!"

Ron and Sue Lambeth and Joe Latimer. Tentmakers. Missionaries. Tentmaker missionaries. A few of a growing army. The Christian movement worldwide could use many more people like them.

What is a Tentmaker?

I was sitting in an airport recently when a man came up as I was working on this manuscript. "What are you writing about?" he asked. He happened to glance at my notes and caught the word "tentmaker." "Oh! Tentmaking!" he said. "You mean like the apostle Paul?"

No context, nothing but the word "tentmaker,"

and this man knew what I was talking about:
"Tentmaking . . . like the apostle Paul."

Tentmaking. The concept is so well-known, it
hardly seems to require explanation. In Acts 18:3,
we read that Paul made tents for a living while he
preached the gospel. In recent years, as a salute to
Paul, the word "tentmaker" has been used to de-
scribe anyone who, like Paul, works at a secular job
in order to support his or her Christian witness.

Originally applied to Christians who live and
work overseas, it has now become possible for some
people to suggest that all Christians who work at
secular jobs are tentmakers. "You don't have to be
an evangelist, and you certainly don't have to live
overseas," they say. "As long as you're living for
Christ, you're a witness, and if you are earning your
own living rather than being supported, then
you're a tentmaker."

I imagine there is some value to such a loose definition. But by and large, it does more to muddy
the waters than to clear them up. I don't want to
detract from the need for people who live for Christ
on the job. But a person who "lives for Christ"
here or overseas is not a tentmaker in the sense we
mean in this book!

As used in this book, the term "tentmaker" refers
to a Christian who works in a cross-cultural situation, is recognized by members of the host culture
as something other than a "religious professional,"
and yet, in terms of his or her commitment, calling,
motivation, and training, is "missionary" in every
way.

Tentmakers are people who cross cultural barriers. They may be found in their home countries

or "overseas," but wherever they may be geographically, in terms of culture they are far from home.

Tentmakers are recognized by members of their host cultures as something other than "religious professionals." They are legally recognized on their visas and in government documents as something other than ministers or missionariers; and socially, though they openly admit to holding strong religious interests and convictions, they validate their presence in their host cultures through interests, skills, or products other than religion.

Finally, in commitment, calling, motivation, and training, tentmakers are "missionary" in every way.

Making a Difference

There are well over a million self-proclaimed American evangelicals living overseas right now. Few have an interest in proclaiming Christ to the people around them. Sure, many of them want to "live for Christ"; they want to "be a good testimony." But their purpose and motivation for being overseas, the reason they have taken the jobs they have, has little to do with the spread of the gospel—and, indeed, their presence overseas has little impact upon the nationals with whom they come in contact.

Darrell, one of the tentmakers we surveyed, said one of the biggest difficulties he and his wife had was "trying to open the eyes of the expatriate Christians to the role they can play in achieving the Great Commission."

Linda and her husband were disappointed to discover how many of the evangelical believers with whom they fellowshipped—even in Saudi Arabia where they were—had little or no vision for ministry. "A deep challenge is needed not only for Christians about to go overseas but for those already overseas to commit themselves fully to working for God's kingdom," Linda said.

Tentmakers are not evangelical Christians who happen to live overseas. Preaching the Gospel is not their "sideline." Tentmakers have a missionary purpose, motivation, and training. They are missionaries.

In "Let's Re-Examine the Tentmaker Myth," an article that appeared in the November 1983 issue of *Moody Monthly* magazine, Don Hillis put it well: "When Jesus Christ ordered believers to 'beseech the Lord of the harvest to send out workers into His harvest,' He was thinking of something more than men and women who moonlight for Him."

Tentmakers are not tentmakers in order to escape the rigors of missionary service. Successful tentmakers don't go as tentmakers in order to avoid raising support, or to escape having to spend the time and money necessary to become thoroughly trained in the scriptures. Their motive for crossing cultural barriers is not to gain additional financial rewards, to advance their careers, or because it sounds dangerous, challenging, exciting, or romantic. Tentmakers become tentmakers because God has called them to use that strategy for lighting a darkened corner (Phil. 2:15).

Jobs Overseas: Strategic Resources for God's Use
Though Hillis was correct in his article about the need for harvest workers who take their job seri-

ously, in general he was too negative about the prospects of tentmaking. "Tentmaking may provide a wedge for getting into closed countries," he said, "(but) worldwide evangelization was never meant to be accomplished this way . . . . The task must be completed by believer-supported prophets, evangelists, and pastor-teachers, not carpenters, fishermen, and tentmakers."

However, biblical evidence and the testimony of countless missionaries over the years makes one realize that self-support is far more than a second-best, wedge-making option in places where church-supported missionaries are unable to gain access.

Successful tentmakers realize their jobs are not "necessary evils" that get in the way of ministry. Rather, they are means to an end, strategic resources to be used for accomplishing God's purposes—purposes that might not otherwise be fulfilled.

William Carey, the father of the modern protestant mission movement, was a tentmaker *par excellence*. A shoemaker, a naturalist, a professor of oriental languages, and, for a time, a government translator, he managed an indigo factory and was one of the most respected botanists and horticulturists in all of Asia. In 1821 he founded the Agricultural and Horticultural Society of India.

He wrote, "We have ever held it to be an essential principle in the conduct of missions, that whenever it is practicable, missionaries should support themselves in whole or in part through their own exertion" (from Sir Kenneth Grubb, "Laymen Abroad," *Frontier* magazine, vol. 4, no. 4, Winter 1961). One of the earliest and most fruitful Protestant mission movements was launched by the Moravians of the 17th century. All of their missionaries supported themselves through secular occupations. Other men and women at the forefront of the Protestant mission movement also used what has come to be known as tentmaking strategy. Mission historians don't often think of them as tentmakers, but applying today's terminology to what they did, that is exactly what they were. Robert Morrison was an interpreter for the East India Company in China. Johannes Emde was a watchmaker in Indonesia. Gladys Aylward was a hotelier.

Models of Godly Living

Even for Paul, tentmaking was not an occasional, second-best option he chose out of necessity when other means of support were unavailable. It was a central part of his strategy for reaching the nations.

In 2 Thessalonians 3:7-9 (see also Acts 20:33-35 and 1 Thess. 4:11, 12) he says, "You yourselves know how you ought to follow our example. We were not idle when we were with you, nor did we eat anyone's food without paying for it. On the contrary, we worked night and day, laboring and toiling so that we would not be a burden to any of you." He explains that he did this, "not because we do not have the right to such help, *but in order to make ourselves a model for you to follow.*"

Bill Bowman, one of the respondents to our survey, worked in Taiwan for two terms as a church-supported missionary before becoming a tentmaker. He said he had been satisfied with his role as a teacher and church planter, and felt he had been a good example in spiritual matters, but he had always been uneasy in the area of finances. Whenever he was asked what he did for a living, he replied that concerned Christians in America were supporting him while he shared the Gospel.

"Yes," said the Taiwanese, "but what do you do for a living?" They couldn't understand the mysterious money faucet Bill turned on whenever he had a need.

Bill said it reminded him of a request Jerry, his four year old son, once made. "Dad," said Jerry, "You know what I want for my birthday?"

"No, what?"

"I want a wallet."

"Oh?" said Bill. "Why's that?"

"Because that's where money comes from," said Jerry. "Anytime you want to buy something, you get money from your wallet. I want one of those!"

Tentmakers can provide new believers with an example of what it means to be a Christian in the work-a-day world, a model that church-supported missionaries are ill-equipped to provide.

To unbelievers, tentmakers provide realistic and believable examples of what Christianity is really all about. Dr. Ronnie Holland, a missionary in Quetta, Pakistan, is reported to have said, "Would to God there were tentmakers here! If nationals see holiness in me, they think I'm a paid religionist like their Muslim leaders. But to see faith and hear the Gospel from an agricultural extension worker on a tractor has greater impact."

Entering for Service

Besides the benefits of a tentmaking approach *per se*, tentmakers are able to enter countries and gain the confidence of people who would otherwise be cut off from a gospel witness.

Half the world's population lives in countries that are officially "off-limits" to those with "Missionary" stamped on their passports. Tentmaker missionaries, however, legally and ethically enter these countries with other purposes than evangelization, church-planting, or Bible translation shown on their passports.

Church supported missionaries generally have had a difficult time reaching out to the business, professional, governmental, and scholarly segments of society. Their social roles limit their effectiveness among such people. Tentmaking professionals, however, can provide a needed witness among these people.

Many people in other cultures think that "American" and "Christian" are synonymous. They mistake the lifestyle of the average American expatriate—including the drinking, the carousing, the loose morals, and cultural pride—as being part of the Christian norm! Certainly, with jobs abounding overseas for "Christian" Americans—there are currently 3 to 4 million Americans living and working overseas—it seems it would be better for the overall witness of the Gospel if committed Christians, rather than atheists or nominal believers, occupy these positions.

Worldwide, there are approximately 130,000 full-time cross-cultural missionaries. The needs are so great among many people who have already been evangelized, however, that only 10 to 15 percent of these missionaries, between 13,000 and 20,000 people, are working among cultural groups that have no other viable Christian witness. Eighty-five to 90 percent of all missionaries are working in cultures where Christian movements have already been established. They are engaged in what the U.S. Center for World Mission calls "inter-church aid" or support ministry.

Think of it. Here in North America, with a total population of less than 270 million, and a total evangelical population of close to 60 million, we have a million full-time Christian workers—a ratio of better than one full-time Christian worker for every 300 members of the population; better than one evangelical for every five members of the general populace.

Realizing this as the ratio of Christians and Christian workers to the population of the United Sates, how many Christians (missionaries) do you think we should send to adequately evangelize the populations of countries where there are no indigenous Christian movements already established? Should we send one missionary for every 100,000 people? One per 75,000? 50,000? 10,000? 2,000?

If we were to send just one missionary couple for every 10,000 people in the Hindu, Chinese, and Muslim worlds, we would need 250,000 couples, 500,000 people—nearly four times the entire worldwide mission force today!

Hundreds of thousands of evangelicals already work in countries and among peoples that are "off-limits" to missionary outreach. If they were properly trained and had the appropriate motivation, they could provide many of the resources for which the mission industry is looking.

Pitfalls in Tentmaking

Despite the advantages a tentmaking strategy can offer, people who have been on the field report several pitfalls. Both tentmakers and more traditional church-supported missionaries point out several areas in which tentmakers appear to be weak:

1) Tentmakers tend to be mavericks, lone rangers. They go out to the field to "do their own thing" with no thought of how they might link up with ministries already in place when they arrive.

Lacking a larger or longer-term strategy than what they hope to achieve on their own, with no support team, no reporting structure, no accountability, and no consultation with or authorization from anyone but themselves, they often wind up, at best, achieving no measurable positive ends, and at worst, creating problems for themselves and other Christians in their vicinity.

2) Tentmakers go to the field biblically or spiritually ill-equipped. They lack the training, background, or other resources to handle the spiritual issues with which they are confronted.

3) Tentmakers often place a low priority on learning to use the local language.

4) Tentmakers' jobs take so much of their time and energy that their ministries are subverted.

But these are not tentmakers by our definition. They may be evangelical Christians overseas, but they are not tentmakers. Remember, tentmakers are missionaries, like the Apostle Paul. Missionaries are not mavericks, lone rangers, without reporting structure, without accountability, ill-equipped in biblical training, without commitment to learn the local language. Neither are tentmakers.

The following chapters, I pray, will help motivate you to prepare for a successful tentmaking ministry. You need to do everything possible to avoid these pitfalls.

Questions for Study and Discussion

1. In your own words, what is a tentmaker?

2. What are your motives for wanting to become a tentmaker?
3. What advantages does church-support have over self-support—and in what circumstances? What advantages does self-support have over church support—and in what circumstances?

4. What weaknesses are you most likely to display if you should become a tentmaker?

5. From the evidence provided, what things did Joe Latimer do that contributed to his success in China?

Knowing that God has called
you is absolutely necessary
at times of frustration and
discouragement. If you're
going to be successful, you'd
better have an unwavering
belief that God is the one
who sent you — not a
mission organization, job,
or anything else.

Cheryl

CHAPTER TWO

You Need to Know God's Will and Be Committed to Doing It

L isten to anyone who's been a successful tentmaker and you'll have no
doubts that tentmaking can be a wonderfully re-
warding experience.

Phil Potter worked in southern Asia as a tentmaker. "God used me to plant a church in a pre-
dominantly Hindu village," he wrote. "That is
more gratifying to me than working in the U.S. for
any luxury."

Bill Near said he didn't know if the success he
and his wife Cathy experienced during their year in
Beijing was because of their particular positions or
the ripeness of the "sector" with which they
worked. Still, he said, "Seventeen P.R.C. Chinese
became Christians by our leading. That astounds
us . . . ."

John Warner, one of several tentmakers we con-
tacted in the Middle East, said he doesn't measure
the effectiveness or success of his time overseas "by
the number of people I was ministering to, but rather, the quality of the lives of the two or three I was
able to help personally, and their convictions and
maturity that are now causing them to pass on to
others what I shared with them."

Bob and Ruth Allman said their ministry impacted more than just nationals. "Our areas of sharing included international people from many different nations, fellow Americans living overseas (not tentmaker Christians), 'established' tentmaking missionaries, and of course the nationals of the land."

Self Growth

Successful tentmakers testified that their times overseas not only made an impact in the lives of the people around them, but also in their own lives.

"I grew in faith more in my two and a half years overseas as a tentmaker than in my previous 10 years as a Christian," Greg wrote.

Linda said, "My initial two-year tentmaking experience was life-changing. It was difficult to come home and be expected to be as I had been. I couldn't be the same: my priorities were different; my compassion for people was greater; and the materialism of America was suddenly rather offensive. I feel I am a better World Christian now. God is teaching me much."

The Cost of Tentmaking

Tentmaking has its rewards. It can also destroy you. You need to count the cost.

"My wife hated tentmaking!" George exclaimed. "Now she is bitter, and the experience has hurt our marriage. She was very unprepared for life overseas. She thought she'd do okay, but with no preparation, she was quite shocked after just a few weeks."

Phyllis said a friend of hers went as a missionary, "became an English teacher to earn a living, folded under the pressure, and fell away from the Lord."

"We came overseas to be tentmakers in China," wrote Alice. "My husband changed his mind and, seemingly, some of his priorities, and decided to go into business. The influence of a strongly anti-Christian culture and the lack of accountability and Christian fellowship made him stumble."

Tentmaking may be costly for you in the way it was costly for these people. I pray that, though for a time they may be derailed, in the end they will come back on track. Still, far better that they should have paid a price for a purpose—that they could have accomplished something good for the kingdom of God!

If you want to be successful, tentmaking will always be costly in terms of commitment. Successful tentmakers are not only committed to spend the time necessary to prepare themselves for ministry before they go, but they are willing to work, watch, wait, and pray for the development of relationships once they get to their destination. Their success comes through a testimony borne in the midst of long-term relationships and shared experiences.

"Tentmaking is not for those who are looking for a short-cut to the mission field," said Dick. "I am convinced that having an effective ministry as a tentmaker is considerably more difficult than being effective as a professional missionary. This is not to say that I am not sold on the tentmaker concept. I am. It is simply to agree with Greg Livingstone (founder of Frontiers, a mission to Muslims) that the only kind of people who can have a significant impact as tentmakers are 'unstoppables.'"

Sherri confessed that she wasn't prepared for the kind of time commitment successful tentmaking required. "It takes years (at least one-and-a-half to two) before a tentmaker has been around long enough for nationals to trust and befriend them. By that time I had just about lost hope, and was lonely and worn out. Maybe someone else can take it, but it was too much for me."

"Americans are in too big a hurry for fruit," Paul said. "They forget that it takes nine months for a child to be born and at least two or three years for trees to produce fruit. Every farmer prepares the ground before planting, and a field fallowed for years takes *a lot of work*. There are few short cuts. Plan on taking at least a year or two before seeing anything significant happen."

Ruth said, "I am now finding with just over 3 years here that my effectiveness is increasing because of greater language proficiency, a wider network of contacts, and more confidence in my work and witness."

Vern minced no words: "There's no such thing as Christian magic. It takes time. Quick, cute answers are no help and *The Four Spiritual Laws* aren't guaranteed. One is naive to think he can just land a job overseas, move there, and jump into an effective ministry. It takes an all-out long term commitment."

Vonna counseled, "Don't rush into witness but stay in prayer about each person and when to talk to them about the Lord. Americans can tend to come on too strong. Wait on the Lord and see Him work. Truly love the people the Lord gives you and they will see that love and respond to it. Above all, take time to do things and be with people. Often at those times opportunities to talk come up naturally."

Knowing God's Will

If you're going to pay the price to be a successful tentmaker; if you're going to invest the time and energy necessary to make adequate preparation; if you are going to wait on the Lord for the doors of opportunity to enter a country, and then for the fruit you hope to bear once you're there; you'll have to be convinced it is God's will for you to be a tentmaker. You'll have to be solidly committed to achieving his will through your life.

Bill said, "If you're going for the sense of adventure or the novelty of an overseas experience, forget it. Adventure and novelty wear off too fast."

Jody added, "Without a sense of service, you'd go crazy in the seeming meaninglessness and frustration of some of your tasks. If you lack a clear sense of God's calling, it is easy to doubt and to wonder why on earth you ever went. Your ministry must be the result of God's directing, a response of 'woe is me if I disobey when He says "go"'!"

"Knowing that God has called you is absolutely necessary at times of frustration and discouragement," said Cheryl. "If you're going to be successful, you'd better have an unwavering belief that *God* is the one who sent you—not a mission organization, job, or anything else."

Fred agreed: "Personal knowledge that God is calling you is most important. In my case, all the other preparations were secondary."

My Introduction to Missions

After graduating from the University of Missouri in 1942, I moved up the corporate ladder until I was a division manager with Xerox Corporation. One day in 1973, Ralph Winter called me. He said that he and six other mission strategists had been meeting since July of 1971, asking God for the right man to start a new organization that would fill in the missing links in missions. He wondered if I would consider such a position.

After meeting with Winter and his friends, Charlotte, my wife, and I began to pray. I was meeting with a group of dedicated Christian men for Bible study and prayer, and I asked them to pray with us as well.

At the time, Charlotte and I happened to be reading the story of Esther— how the Jews were threatened with extinction if a plot to destroy them had not been exposed and steps taken to counter-balance the threat. Esther the queen was asked by her uncle, Mordecai, to appeal to the king on behalf of the Jewish people.

"But I can't go!" Esther said. "The king hasn't asked me to come into his presence for a month, and I'll be killed if I go in to talk with him without his asking me to come. If he doesn't raise his scepter to me, I'm done for."

"Do you think that just because you are queen you will be spared the slaughter intended for the Jewish people?" Mordecai asks. "If you don't go, then a deliverer will be raised from some other source. But perhaps you have come into the kingdom for such a time as this?"

Esther decides Mordecai is probably right. She

asks him to gather all the Jews living in the capital
city at that time to fast for her for three days.
"When this is done," she says, "I will go to the king,
even though it is against the law. And if I perish, I
perish."

As Charlotte and I prayed about our situation, I
thought there was a real parallel. American busi-
nesses are on the lookout for people with continu-
ous records of progress. They don't want someone
with two year or longer side-tracks into missions. If
I were to accept the offer of the mission strategists, I
faced a "perish" situation. My career could be
ruined.

Despite the risks, it was soon clear what Charlotte's and my decision would be. We felt God
wanted us to go with Winter and the other men
and start the William Carey Institute. I told them
our decision.

And then, the very next morning, I received a
call from New York. It was from an executive re-
cruiter, a "corporate head hunter;" he wanted to
talk with me about an outstanding opportunity.

"Thanks anyway," I said. But then my advisors
suggested I should at least consider his offer. I
called him back.

When he came to Los Angeles, he told me he
had a position for me as the general manager of a
$50 million company. I'd have 20 percent owner-
ship and a six-figure salary.

Now what? Our mission friends would give me
no advice. Pete Wagner, one of the group, said, "I
won't touch that one with a ten foot pole—that's
your problem."

Charlotte and I wrestled in prayer.

"With that kind of salary and with our priorities and lifestyle already settled, look what we could do for missions! Why, we could give more than whole churches to the cause of Christ," I said.

"Yes, but . . . ."

As we studied the scriptures, God led us to Psalm 50:10—"I own the cattle on a thousand hills." I own all the wealth of the world. What I want is *you*. Are you going to obey me or not? The next morning I called the head hunter.

"I'm sorry," I began, "but after praying about your offer . . . ."

"Oh!" he interrupted. "I'm so glad you called. You know, while I was on the west coast I met with another man who is even better qualified. I offered him the job and he accepted on the spot!"

Many times in the years that followed it was nothing more than the absolute conviction that it was God's will for our lives to be there that kept us working at the William Carey Institute and the Association of Church Missions Committees (ACMC), the first new organization started by the Institute.

It is just as important for tentmakers to be convinced God has called them to serve where they are as it was for Charlotte and me to be convinced he wanted us at WCI. It may be even more important for tentmakers than it was for us, since tentmakers commonly enjoy less field support than Charlotte and I had.

Why give this example of one who moved from a full-time secular job to one in missions? Simply to emphasize the crucial importance of listening to and obeying God's will. The example of Bill Bowman, discussed above, who went from a missionary to a tentmaker, is just as impressive a story from the other perspective. Many with InterServe (formerly BMMF) have gone from tentmaker to missionary and back to tentmaker, depending on the circumstances and specific leading of the Lord. The important point: be obedient to God's leading.

Questions for Study and Discussion

1) Have you determined for sure that God wants you to become a tentmaker?

2) If so, what costs will you have to pay in order to be a successful tentmaker?

3) Jesus told His disciples to count the cost of following Him: are you willing to pay it? If you are, sign your name here and write the date.

4) If not, what reasons do you have to think God may want you to become a tentmaker?

5) What reasons do you have to think God may NOT want you to become a tentmaker?

6) What evidence will convince you of God's will in the matter?

7) Write out a plan of action you intend to follow in order to acquire the evidence you need to come to a firm decision in this matter; share that plan with someone who is intimately concerned for your welfare and productivity in service to God; ask

for their commitment to hold you accountable to the plan.

Write here the date you complete the above steps.

If you haven't learned how to share your faith, lead someone to Christ, and help him grow in your own country — overseas isn't the place to learn. It's 100 times harder out of your own culture.

— George

CHAPTER THREE

You Need to be Spiritually Qualified

S oon after the first group of Christian teachers arrived in Afghanistan in the late 1940s, some of them felt they needed to pray as a group. When they got together, Harry led off. As he started to pray, the table began to shake; bowls, papers, and other objects fell to the floor. Some unknown power forced Harry to stop praying. Try as he would, he could not begin again.

There was a deathly silence in the room as the teachers glanced at one another nervously. The hair on their necks stood on end. Unsure of what was happening or how to proceed, they finally decided to gather around Harry, lay their hands on him, and try praying again.

"Lord!" they cried. "Help us!"

In the name of the Lord Jesus Christ, they prayed that any demonic powers in that room would be forced to scatter. The oppressive atmosphere began to dissipate and Harry was able to pray once more.

You Need Skills and Ability in Spiritual Warfare

Most American evangelicals are woefully unaware of satanic influences and wholly inexperienced in dealing with them. Many tentmakers we

31

surveyed said ignorance in this area meant almost a paralyzing defeat in ministry.

"You need to be aware of 'spiritual warfare' and supernatural manifestations; i.e. healings, power encounters, etc.," said Nancy.

Scott agreed. "If you don't know how to do spiritual battle, you're in for trouble," he said. "Be prepared to deal with evil spirits. Be aware that another has had the field and won't want to let go of it."

Ron, too, said, "Much prayer support is necessary—especially because of demonic activities."

Jane said she and her husband were not adequately prepared spiritually. "Spiritually, we have faced a lot of darts from the Devil. He isn't happy with our work."

On the positive side, Ruth commented, "The closer we walk with the Lord, the harder the enemy attacks, but 1 John 4:4—'greater is He who is in us than he who is in the world'—proves true every time."

"Your relationship with God is the Number One most important thing you can have on the field," Dick, a tentmaker in his early 50s, agreed. "Your relationship with God must be deep, intimate, and abiding. It is essential to know the very heart-beat of God—and even then you are likely to be shaken." Dick was not alone in his belief concerning the importance of having a strong personal relationship with God. More tentmakers commented about this matter than anything else except for ministry experience and prayer support. Skill and ability in spiritual warfare are rooted in one's relationship with God.

You Need to Have a Good Relationship With God

Neil stated the obvious: if you plan to introduce other people to Jesus, then you need to know him yourself first! "Your own personal relationship with the Lord is paramount to sharing him effectively anywhere."

Several others went a step further: having a strong personal relationship with the Lord is necessary not merely for success as a witness, but for mere survival.

"The lack of privacy and extreme noise made the living situation very difficult for my wife and me, Ron confessed. "The school which I worked for did not honor their contract. Responsibilities and wages changed at the whim of the administration. I know now that a deeper walk with the Lord would have enabled me to cope better."

Shirley, a former tentmaker in China, asserted, "The pressures of the world overseas seem even more intense than here in the States, and weariness and confusion make it harder, so you must be growing in your relationship with the Lord before you go, and have a plan to continue to grow."

Earle said, "Stress is greater in a foreign culture. If a person is going to be able to pick himself up and go on when he fails, he has to have a learning attitude, flexibility, and a good self-image. These come from a close daily relationship with God."

"A person must already have established sound habits before going," wrote Esther. "Prayer, daily personal exposure to God's Word, and being sensitive to the Holy Spirit on a moment-by-moment basis is vital."

Mary said almost the same thing: "You must

have a good foundation in the scriptures, you must know how to use the scriptures to solve problems, and you must know the power of prayer."

"When you're in a place like I am, you need to know Jesus well and know how to get to know God more intimately on your own," Richard, a tentmaker in a Middle Eastern country, commented. "You need to be able to feed yourself spiritually and function on your own without props."

"Being overseas forced me more and more to realize my security is in the Lord and not my country, not my culture, not even my family," said Ken. "The Lord alone is my stability."

Prayer

"Prayer is vital to operate where Satan is opposing us," said Susan. "Rather than a seminar or lecture on these matters, a person needs a program in which he/she can develop the necessary disciplines."

Andy urged that, especially on account of demonic activity, one should "pray with other Christians!"

Bob is convinced he would have been more effective had he been more faithful in prayer. "Not prayer as usual, but intense disciplined prayer."

Daily, Personal Exposure to God's Word

Sharon added, "God's Word is our life: without it—and him—we can do nothing."

Muriel, still on the field in North Africa, agreed. "You need to be firmly rooted in the Word," she said. By way of warning to prospective tentmakers, she added, "Be aware. Satan attacks us mostly in devotional time."

Being Sensitive to God's Spirit

"Without the Holy Spirit as my constant companion and guide, giving me wisdom not my own, I would have done a lot of foolhardy things," said Sarah.

Victor said, "A total submission to the Holy Spirit and constant filling by him—a crucified life (Gal. 2:20)—is the means for a powerful ministry."

If you have any doubts about your relationship with God, that is the first step to preparation as a tentmaker. If you're in need in this area, find help before you try moving ahead another step.

You Need to Have Wisdom and Maturity

Many people think having a personal relationship with God is enough. With one voice, virtually all the tentmakers who responded to our survey disagreed with that idea. They said they needed more knowledge of the scriptures than a regular quiet time alone would provide. Saturation with scriptural truth is vital.

"Get all the Bible preparation you can," they said. "It is essential not only for effective ministry, but for personal survival." Just because you as a tentmaker may have no agency requiring such biblical preparation, doesn't mean you don't need it. Many tentmakers said they felt their biblical and spiritual preparation should have been on a par with or even exceeded that of more traditional, fully-supported missionaries.

You Need Quality Training in the Scriptures

James, a man in his mid-30s declared, "When surrounded by the majority of people who believe something opposed to Christianity, it's easy for one's faith to be shaken. I came closest to leaving the faith during my time as a tentmaker. It's extremely important to have good grounding in Bible and theology."

Phyllis said, "Many cultures that previously have been exposed to Christianity have heretical teachings—it seems like the cults always get there first. Without a good Bible background you can get as confused as the ones you are trying to minister to."

Hal said he and his wife, Judy, found they were forced to learn anew what biblical Christianity is. They had come to know an "American or campus group Christianity." They needed something else. "We could not just rely on our past experiences," Hal said. "We were forced to refer to biblical *principles*. You'd better have solid Biblical convictions and not convictions that are, in reality, religious traditions from your particular background or denomination."

"Think about why you believe," Bob suggested. "Why are you not an atheist? What role does Christianity play in the health of a nation? What are the results of other religions on society?"

Chris, a young man who is still on the field, confessed he is finding his lack of scripture knowledge a real hindrance to ministry. "Be as prepared as you can be before you go," he pleaded. "There is not enough time on the field to develop your biblical approach."

"My husband and I missed out on a lot of opportunities while we were overseas because we had not prepared ourselves adequately in the area of biblical training," said Melanie.

Finding the Source

But where, when, and how should one go about getting such training? And how much preparation is necessary? On these matters there was some disagreement.

"I'm so glad that my husband and I have seminary training behind us," Jill said. "It's irreplaceable on the mission field. In fact, it's essential."

"I'd definitely recommend attending a seminary," John agreed, "—a seminary with a strong emphasis on cross-cultural ministry."

Phil was of a different opinion. "(While) there is absolutely no substitute for thorough biblical and spiritual preparation," he said, "the training offered by the Navigators or IVCF or Campus Crusade in the context of a campus ministry might be preferable to a seminary or Bible school background."

Along similar lines, Connie said, "Formal Bible training is not necessary as long as one has a good working knowledge of the Word and has had adequate training in ministry. A tentmaker should have practical experience in his own culture before going overseas."

"The emphasis should be on spiritual truths applied to daily life, and not just head knowledge or a degree from a Bible school," said Terry. "Christ-like character and the fruit of the Spirit must be evident in a tentmaker's life."

Mary was of the same opinion: "Know as much of the Word of God as possible, but most important, be led of the Spirit of God in all situations. Remember, you came in his strength and it is in his strength you are upheld. His Word does not return void!"

37

Fully Equipped

And that, really, is the end of the matter. You must know God's Word in your head, but it must also be stored in your heart and working its way out in your life.

Clyde said, "Get as much preparation as a well-prepared missionary, but don't wait until you feel you are 'spiritually qualified.' Everyone falls short. Go when God says 'go.' Follow when He says 'follow.' Supplement biblical training with practical cross-cultural application. Don't get bogged down in an 'over-preparation' syndrome; it will only squelch your zeal for Jesus."

Don, one of the older and more experienced tentmakers we surveyed, commented, "Planning, preparation, and placement is important, but moving out and getting involved is more so. If the Lord is thrusting you out immediately, go!! Get all the preparation you can, but don't look for or use any excuses not to go, or to delay going."

He suggested that perhaps people should become tentmakers in stages: "At each stage, they could get both more secular training and more Bible and cross-cultural training."

"If you wait until you're totally ready, you'll never go," he said. "The important thing is to have enough training to have a good first experience (so you'll want to go back), and, at the same time, to have encouragement to keep improving."

There is a balance. On the one hand, it is easy to keep preparing so long that you never get there. On the other, most of the tentmakers who failed failed because they lacked the theoretical and practical knowledge of the scriptures that would have allowed them to meet the needs of the people with whom they were working. The main point: *Don't cop-out, but be sure you can cope!*

You Need a Solid Background of Ministry Experience

Beyond biblical knowledge, another foundation that was stressed over and over again was the need to *get ministry experience before going overseas.* Get experience on campus, in church, in evangelistic Bible studies, in ministry to international students, in life, . . . anywhere . . . —but *get experience.*

George commented, "If you haven't learned how to share your faith, lead someone to Christ, and help him grow in your own country—overseas isn't the place to learn. It's 100 times harder out of your own culture."

"I really feel the lack of never having been in a discipleship program, or evangelistic training," said Tony. "It meant I didn't know how to go about it myself once I was overseas. I definitely encourage a tentmaker to participate in one or both of these before going."

Tom claimed his background with Inter-Varsity made him "automatically look at the place where I was as a mission field." Further, "having experience ministering in a campus situation and then in the working world gave me the confidence I needed to minister overseas."

However, as good as campus ministries may be, ministry among others of a similar age, race, and social group may not be enough. Several people said you should also have experience in doing cross-cultural evangelism.

"Work with foreign students helped me a lot," said Bill. "Foreigners see things a lot differently! I think my time visiting the local mosque was most helpful, because, while still physically in the United States, I was someone else's guest, and on their turf."

Janice added: "Getting to know international students is a great way to experience what it is like to relate to a person from another culture. Also you can really serve these people while they are away from home."

"International student ministry, ethnic ministry, and refugee outreach at home is excellent preparation," said Linda.

Paul said you should "embrace in your own culture the type of things God is doing among the people you will work with overseas. If going to Latin America, for instance, get in touch with charismatics, and become involved immediately with Catholics."

With all the other comments about ministry experience, however, there was one type of experience that stood head and shoulders above the others in terms of importance. A full 98 percent of those who rated very good to excellent as tentmakers had led evangelistic Bible studies before going overseas, and those who had that background commented on it.

Darrell was fairly typical when he said, "I was glad I had experience leading Bible study groups before I went overseas. It meant I had tools I could use with confidence. It also meant I had tools I could pass on to those I was teaching so they could have a ministry rooted in the Word once I left."

In most areas where tentmakers operate, one cannot pass out tracts, go door-to-door, or hold evangelistic meetings. Those who have conducted evangelistic Bible studies are best prepared to establish one-on-one relationships and then, as questions are asked, to share their faith in Christ. They have the biblical background; they have experience in explaining the answers to questions and helping others to think critically for themselves. According to our survey, to attend such an evangelistic Bible study is good, but far better is to have led one successfully.

Questions for Study and Discussion

1. Many missionaries have learned to live and operate in an environment where spiritual warfare is blatant. Seek out some missionaries and ask them what experience they have had in dealing with demonic powers. What principles have they learned? What scriptures have been helpful to them?

2. What plans do you have for increasing your intimacy with God? Write them down and share them with a friend. Ask your friend for support in pursuing your plans. Write the date and sign your name in the margin of the book as soon as you have found a friend who will support you in this manner. (Now pursue your plan!)

3. What plans do you have for increasing your knowledge of scripture? Where can you receive

quality training in this area?

4. Why do you think leading an evangelistic Bible study is such an important experience for a person to become an effective tentmaker?

5. What kind of ministry experience can you acquire in the next 12 months? Make a list of all the options. Which experiences could include people from other cultures?

6. Talk to your spiritual leaders about getting biblical training and ministry experience. Talk with them about your purposes and goals. Ask them for their recommendations, help, and encouragement. Make a plan and follow it.

Even if you read the entire Bible daily and pray from midnight to dawn, don't go alone! I repeat,

DON'T GO ALONE.

—Jerry

CHAPTER FOUR

You Need a Team

One day, so the story goes, Satan held an auction of all his tools. The array was stunning: sickness, death, natural disasters, unconfessed sin, unfaithful friends, hypocrites in the church . . . . All were on display, all were for sale.

In the farthest corner of the room, behind a stack of greed and lust, there lay an old, well-worn instrument. It had no price tag.

"How much do you want for this one?" an eager demon asked.

"Sorry," Satan replied, "that one's not for sale."

Another demon, overhearing the interchange, asked what the tool was used for.

"It's one of a kind," said Satan, fingering it lovingly. "There's nothing else like it. I can defeat more Christians with this than anything else. It's called Discouragement."

Listening to tentmakers, you'd have to agree. Discouragement is one of the most effective weapons in Satan's arsenal.

"God has since re-established my relationship with him, and my wife and I intend to return to the field," wrote Tim, "but the discouragements we faced while we were in North Africa strained our relationship and caused a period of backsliding."

God has made his people to work as a connected body (1 Corinthians 12). Even if you have the deepest commitment to the Lord, daily devotions, a regular prayer life, and more scripture knowledge than the best seminary professor, you still need human aid if you're going to stay on track as a tentmaker and avoid the paralysis of discouragement.

Prayer Warriors

One of the most important types of help you can get comes in the form of prayer.

"We had people who committed themselves to pray for us each week so we were upheld each day," Paul said. "(We found) that is a key to enculturation, energy, and spiritual fruit."

Bill wrote, "There were many times when knowing I had a team of prayer partners buoyed me up."

"My home church has not shown the interest I thought it would, and I've really felt it!" said Donna. Jerry said he wanted to be placed on his church's missionary prayer list. He went to the mission committee and was rebuffed.

"Sorry," said the committee chairman, "but we only put missionaries we're supporting on that list."

"Well," Jerry responded, "what if you support me at negative $100 per month? I'll send you $100 a month to pray for me! I need your prayer support."

Gil confessed his lack of adequate prayer support had nothing to do with the church, it was his own fault—he never asked for it. Now he wishes he had been more diligent in seeking that kind of help. "I had moved shortly before going overseas and did not communicate my going overseas to a local church, so I was not directly supported either financially or spiritually. Looking back, I should have asked the church I had gone to while I was at school to commission me as a tentmaker and I should have been accountable to them—and them to me in prayer."

Church Support

If we were to ignore the comments of tentmakers and simply look at the statistics, we would find that effective tentmakers have strong relationships with their home churches. There were 16 questions in the questionnaire having to do with the tentmakers' relationships with their home churches. On *every one* of these questions the very good to excellent tentmakers had higher average scores than less effective or merely average tentmakers.

Effective tentmakers not only believed in the importance of the local church, but they tended to be more regular in attendance; they obtained more of their ministry experience there; it was where they looked for their long-range fellowship and support; it was where they had come to know the Lord. They felt accountable to their churches and reported to them regularly.

They tended to give their churches a higher ranking when it came to support, too. From the perspective of the church, tentmaking was a form of true missionary service: they commissioned their outgoing tentmakers and prayed for them as they did for their conventional missionaries.

Local Team Support

Important as that supportive church back home is, however, its help can only go so far. Many tentmakers indicated they had a support group nearby as well—a "field team" whose presence was vital.

"There are times when vocal reassurance is desperately needed," Ruth confessed. And while, as she put it, "just (having) someone around of your own background, culture, language, etc., is s-o-o-o good and vital," in the long run, that's not good enough.

You need to "seek out other tentmakers to form a support group," Carrie urged. "There were plenty of other expatriates here, but very few who considered themselves tentmakers." Greg said he met some "rather pathetic examples of Christians" while he was overseas. "Some of these fell into sin, lacked guidance and drew away from responsibility," he said. He attributed their problems to "(lack of) proper support or people to be accountable to."

"A team of fellow believers with the same goal and vision is crucial," said Jill. "Without supportive fellowship, I would have fallen and gone astray."

Carl agreed: "I had a close support team of foreigners whom I met with regularly for Bible study, prayer, accountability and fellowship. They were a strength and blessing as they helped me realize I was not alone, and offered me encouragement, support and stimulation. They had as much to do with my tentmaking experience being a success as anything. Without their fellowship I would have been too discouraged to stay."

To have this heart-to-heart relationship of depth

is a big factor in many things, i.e., keeping encouraged, sharpened, challenged, humored, accountable, maintaining perspective," wrote Chuck.

"I would discourage anyone from going anywhere alone," said Phil. "I had a wonderful network of support in Beijing, both an English-speaking church and a Bible study group of students and other tentmakers."

Jim said that for his wife and him, "having support on the field was more important than housing, location, or any other aspect of our move. Other believers are invaluable as a support system and means of working together for a common goal. God has blessed us richly in this area."

"Develop some team or some sense of accountability so that you will stay within the parameters of your goals," urged Al. "You need spiritually close friends to help motivate, encourage, and keep you accountable on a daily basis."

"A godly support group can especially help you maintain your prayer and devotions, and strengthen your walk with Christ," said John.

Carol, who according to her own admission didn't have adequate prayer and fellowship support, said she became "unduly discouraged and depressed by circumstances." "Actually, I became so discouraged, I came closer to leaving the faith during my time as a tentmaker than at any time since I became a Christian."

Al didn't say he was ready to leave the faith, but, "had I been in a team or had Christian fellowship and support, my experience would have been much less discouraging."

Field support is useful not only as a defense

against discouragement and spiritual ruin, but as an aid to effective ministry.

"We had a super missionary couple about 30 kilometers from where we lived," said Gary. "Through deep, meaningful sharing with these people I gained insights that enabled me to share my faith with the Japanese as though I had been there four or six years instead of the two."

Cindy said that almost all the missionaries she and her husband work with "have been tremendously supportive and have made us feel part of 'the team,'" even though "at first (they) made comments to us about us not really being missionaries."

Linda said, "We have sought out relationships with missionaries who could strengthen us in areas of inexperience and who could serve as friends and counselors." Still, "we often have wished for another tentmaking couple with whom to converse and share our unique ministry and goals."

Helping Each Other

Even among tentmakers, though, merely having each other around is not enough. You need to consciously view your relationship in terms of a team. There has to be commitment.

"People tend to get too involved in their own ministries," said Ron. "Just because you are able to work with other missionaries, or there are other tentmakers in the city, doesn't mean there is a team. You have to work at it."

Jerry concluded his comments, and I'll conclude this chapter: "Even if you read the entire Bible daily and pray from midnight to dawn, don't go alone! I repeat, DON'T GO ALONE."

Some Questions for Study and Discussion

1. What is a team good for? List all the reasons the tentmakers said they wanted or needed a team.

2. Can you think of any other reasons you may want a team?

3. What kinds of people would you want on your team? Why would you want them?

4. We've all heard about—or imagined hearing about—the exceptional pioneer missionary who launched out on his own, reported to no one, and did outstanding work for God. On the other hand, we seldom hear about failures on the mission field. Ask the next missionary you meet if he or she would recommend going out alone. Pursue the question one further step: *Why?*

5. A team cannot be put together overnight. As Bob put it, you need to have at least one or two people with whom you can bare your soul. A relationship like that is developed slowly and carefully. What can you do right now to start developing a team? Add at least 10 items to each list.

a. At home.
—Talk to the missions committee.
—Write every month; give them names and needs to pray for.
—Send pictures.

b. For the field.
—Pray for partners.
—Share my vision with friends.

Many Japanese were amazed by the fact that I was "not a missionary" yet still a Christian. It is striking to them that people whose jobs are not 'religion' also believe and act similarly to missionaries.

— Evelyn

CHAPTER FIVE

You Need Social Skills

Experts say the number one reason missionaries leave the field is that they can't get along with their co-workers. Tentmaker missionaries face the same difficulty. If you're going to remain on the field long enough to have an impact, you need to be able to get along with other people—Christians and non-Christians alike, both nationals and expatriates.

Getting Along With Those Who Are Different

"Above all, beware of criticizing or conflicting with other Christian workers/mission-aries," Pam, a tentmaker in North Africa, counseled. "Satan will attack in that area and try to cause dissension among fellow missionaries."

Among the tools suggested to combat relationship problems: transparency; openness; "learning to live in difficult situations without murmuring and complaining;" and "learning how to put up with other peoples' sometimes- glaring shortcomings in a spirit of love."

Dave said that if you're in a place where there are other Christians, "you need to appreciate the contribution of the whole team and, even though the others may fail you, you need to remember you still need each other. Keep your eyes on Jesus and not on the other tentmakers or missionaries in your area. Be forgiving, accepting and don't let anything shock you!"

And when you're dealing with members of another culture, Marvin testified, "you need to go with an attitude of being a learner and not one who knows it all. You need to be open to different ways of doing things. Some will be better, some worse. Be sensitive to the Holy Spirit and to the people around you."

Jackie laid it on the line: "A sensitivity to, and understanding of, the culture of those you are working with is very necessary if you want them to be open to the gospel. If you are unable to open your mind to people's differences and think you and your culture are always right, you'll be ineffective and frustrated."

In a more confessional tone she added, "I've had to fight against my own tendency to think the people with whom I'm working are stupid because they do things differently than I do. I've had to deliberately work at it to come to appreciate their ways of living."

Sam suggested the best way to "work at" coming to appreciate another culture is to get to know yourself. "Become aware of cultural perspectives your target people may have that are in opposition to your own personal views. Decide ahead of time what importance you attach to these differences and how you want to handle them.

"Analyze your convictions to determine if you are allowing non-biblical or non-essential convictions to have a major impact in your way of looking at the world. As much as possible, try to develop non-cultural convictions based on scripture."

Gertrude commented, however, "Having all the right biblical answers is no substitute for love, gentleness, humor, vulnerability and devotion. If people sense sincerity in you, you—and the gospel—will be more readily accepted."

Yes, Jack agreed. Love, gentleness, humor, etc., are important, but they won't always substitute for a solid understanding of the culture. For example, he said, when he first arrived in Japan he didn't realize the importance of "saving face." He decided to be friendly—except it was "friendly" in an American way. He kidded and teased his way into being very unappreciated by the Japanese students he was trying to befriend.

We come full circle. Attitude is important, but you need to commit yourself to learn culture. The more experience you have dealing with other cultures—any culture—before you go, the more effective you will be at learning the culture of the people to whom you want to minister once you get there.

You need to remember and work with the conscious realization that culture can provide a bridge of contact with the people you're trying to reach or it can erect barriers that keep you at arm's length.

Learning the Language

"Okay," you say. "I need to be sensitive to cultural differences and keep them in mind. But what about language-learning? Do I have to learn the language?"

Virtually without exception, the tentmakers we

surveyed agreed: you need to commit yourself to learn the language of the people you hope to reach.

"People respect the effort and are more willing to listen to you as a result," wrote Mildred. "Make every effort to learn the language—at least to speak it." She said that because her husband learned the language, "the nationals looked up to him as someone who cared."

Language learning is important not only because it will earn you respect, but, as Fred put it, it tells them "that you are interested in learning about their society and culture, you're not merely interested in sharing your religion. It helps break down cultural and spiritual barriers."

George figured he didn't need to learn the language since most of the businessmen with whom he was planning to work could speak English. After having been there, however, he confessed that "language is a lot more of a barrier than I realized." No matter what the nationals' ability is in your language, "it's important to them that you attempt to learn theirs."

Nancy had no doubt that she'd need to learn Turkish. The problem is, she said, "most women here do not speak English, and learning Turkish on my own has been a slow process." She feels she would have been much smarter to have studied more about Islam and the Turkish language before she went.

Ninety percent of all the tentmakers we surveyed attempted to learn the local language; the most effective ones were more often successful in learning to speak it.

Ted summed up the message of this chapter: "It

is crucial to go with a willingness to learn the culture, language and, if necessary, business, politics, . . . whatever is important to the people."

Questions for Study and Discussion

1. According to the tentmakers quoted here, why is language and culture learning so important? Make a list.

2. What can you think of on your own as reasons that an understanding of other people's language and culture is so important? Make a list.

3. Where can you obtain some cross-cultural experience now, before you go overseas? What about language-learning opportunities? Write out a plan of action that you can follow that will improve your skills in these areas.

Tentmakers need to accept their professional work as their ministry. The world goes on and at its gut is commerce: that's where people are. It's where they learn values and methods. It's where they gain their satisfaction. It's crucial that you meet them with godly values, methods and satisfaction.

— Jerry

CHAPTER SIX

You Need a Proper Perspective on Job and Ministry

D ick Hart went to Taiwan at the invitation of the government. An executive with an electrical utility in the United States, he was asked to make a survey of Taiwan's power needs and resources. He brought with him 60 other experts. For six months they probed the matter thoroughly.

Dick had more in mind, however, than merely discovering Taiwan's power requirements. He was determined to share his Christian faith. He told some missionaries he met in the area that from 8 to 5, Monday through Friday, his time belonged to his company and the people he met at work. The rest of the time he was available for speaking, teaching, or helping in any way he could with the missionaries' work.

In addition to Dick's work with the missionaries, he carried on a ministry of his own. Before going to Taiwan, he had prepared a booklet that told about his conversion and present walk with Christ. Now that he was in Taiwan, every day, at lunch and dinner, he invited one of his Chinese associates to eat with him. While they ate, Dick shared his testimony. Having worked with these men during the day, he had earned their respect and his testimony was powerful.

A church-supported missionary who was there at the time says that more than 10 years later, the men with whom Dick had worked—a group of people with whom the missionary had had no previous contact—still talked about Dick and the impact he and his testimony had made on them.

Tentmaking is often criticized because "so much of a tentmaker's time is spent on the job, little or no time is left for ministry." As Don Hillis put it in his *Moody Monthly* article, tentmakers are viewed as "men and women who moonlight" for God.

As you've already discovered, I disagree with such a view of tentmaking. The problem is, many of the tentmakers we surveyed complained that, whatever their desires had been before they went overseas, this is what they experienced.

Linda was fairly typical: "Tentmakers need encouragement because their secular work limits the time they can spend in other ministries."

"The time spent in secular employment detracts much from time available to spread the gospel," Harold agreed. "There isn't much time or energy left over for witnessing apart from the job after taking care of living responsibilities. It is frustrating not to have much time for ministry as I knew it at home."

Bob, a former pastor, said he and his wife found it difficult to accept the fact that his job took up the bulk of his time. "That shift in emphasis (from 'ministry' to 'job') was hard to work through."

Job is Ministry

As common as complaints about tentmakers' jobs getting in the way of ministry are, the problems referred to here have less basis in reality than one might assume.

Many of the criticisms leveled against tentmakers are based on false assumptions about how "full-time missionaries" use their time.

In fact, simply because they enjoy a more robust income, some tentmakers have more time for gospel ministry than do their peers among so-called fulltime missionaries. Typically, the lower one's income, the more time one must spend meeting basic survival needs and making ends meet.

A missionary friend of mine was certainly talking about an extreme situation, but the fact remains, his support was so low at one time that he was forced to spend a week carving new buttons for his wife's overcoat.

The fact is, even when traditional missionaries are adequately supported, their time is not all spent in "ministry."

About eight years ago a major mission agency conducted a survey of its missionaries to see what proportion of their time was spent in different activities. They filled out a check chart in which all possible activities were listed—everything from getting dressed and eating to Bible teaching and evangelism. Fully 78 percent of these dedicated missionaries' time was spent on the normal tasks of living—going to market, preparing food, eating, sleeping, washing clothes, etc. For many it was closer to 90 percent. Only 10 to 30 percent of their time was spent in "missionary" work—between 17 and

52 hours per week.

Committed tentmaker missionaries can easily spend 17 hours a week in active ministry, and with a little care and insight, far more of one's time can legitimately be counted as ministerial in nature.

George, an English instructor in China commented, "It seems to me that in spite of being employed intensively full-time, my ministry is about as effective as that of most urban missionaries whose only occupation is their ministry."

I think he's probably right.

Merging Sacred and Secular

Another reason dedicated tentmakers need not be as ineffective as the criticism implies is that the criticism is based on an unbiblical distinction between "sacred" and "secular."

We Westerners tend to think in terms of the work day—a time devoted to our employers and earning money—as a time which has very little or nothing to do with ministry. We think of evenings and weekends as times for family, recreation, worship, and ministry. Scripture, however, makes no such distinction. As one tentmaker reflected, "I came to the place where my work did not prevent a significant ministry. I realized my secular job itself was ministry. There is no such thing as a part-time Christian."

Indeed, if you look carefully at what Harold, Linda, and Bob had to say, you find hints concerning how they solved the apparent dilemma of job *vs* ministry, because despite their concerns, they were all effective tentmakers according to our survey.

Harold said, "There isn't much time or energy

left over for witnessing *apart from* the job (and) *after* taking care of living responsibilities." And Linda: "Secular work limits the time (one) can spend in *other* ministries." Actually, she went on to say, "In addition to encouragement, tentmakers need instruction on how to *integrate* their work and ministry."

Tentmakers are no different from witnesses for Christ in all cultures—even missionaries. Effective witnesses realize that all of life is the Lord's; we are Christians, and God can use us, whatever our occupation.

Darlene, a nurse who worked in a "closed" country said that, until she made that discovery, her tentmaking experience was the most frustrating time of her life. She was required to spend 60 to 70 hours a week in totally exhausting work and "had no time for ministry."

But then one day her colleagues asked her how she did it: "How do you keep up?"

"Jesus helps me," she said.

"'Jesus?'" they asked. "What's that?"

Suddenly she realized that her job had given her a unique opportunity to sensitively and openly share her faith in Christ. Her diligence at work had earned her the right to be heard.

Salt in the Earth

Too often, Westerners underrate the significance of working side-by-side with other people. Bruce said that his working like they did "allowed the nationals to identify" with him.

Chuck, a tentmaker in eastern Europe, commented, "Secular employment limits the time, energy and possibility of 'traditional' ministry. However, since we have become normal, 'ordinary' people in our host culture, other people are open to us in ways they may not be to traditional missionaries. I have to admit, by 'being there' with them, I better understand the life and faith questions of the people I work with!"

Evelyn said that many Japanese were amazed by the fact that she was "not a missionary" yet still a Christian. "It is striking to them that people whose jobs are not 'religion' also believe and act similarly to missionaries," she said.

Emma, a tentmaker in Europe, said it wasn't the fact that she and her family were similar to missionaries that struck the nationals, rather, it was the contrast between how they conducted themselves and the way Americans in general tended to act. "Our primary witness was in lifestyle as a Christian family among so many other Americans with low moral standards."

Jerry said tentmakers need to accept their professional work as their ministry. "The world goes on and at its guts is commerce: that's where people are. It's where they learn values and methods. It's where they gain their satisfaction. It's crucial that you meet them with godly values, methods and satisfaction. Nationals need to see the Christian life lived right before their eyes."

Others said they thought they had an easier time relating to nationals as tentmakers than they would have had as missionaries. They thought it was more natural and more effective. For instance, Dave said his position as a teacher "added credibility" to what he had to say.

Beyond all these things, however, the tentmakers I surveyed said they thought they had more freedom to build relationships with nationals than most church-supported missionaries are likely to have. "Many 'fulltime missionaries' I knew did not have the contacts with people—especially non-Christian people—that I had through my job," said Linda, a nurse in Nairobi, Kenya.

George, who has been both a tentmaker and a salaried missionary, said his two years of tentmaking pulled him into experiences he had been unable to have as a missionary "simply because of the 'missionary' label."

Perhaps we should do away with the distinction between "tentmakers" and "missionaries," a tentmaker from the Muslim world suggested. "Nearly all 'missionaries' in the Middle East have a tentmaker guise, anyway, regardless of their funding sources."

The point is, if a Christian is to be an effective witness for his Lord, no matter what his capacity or what his title, he must learn to integrate his work and ministry because *that is the best way to minister.*

Professionalism is a good basis for witness; it earns the worker the right to be heard; it frees up time for ministry; and, for tentmakers, it provides a means not only for getting into a country, but for staying there and being invited back.

Professionalism Earns the Right to be Heard

Being good at your work is in itself a witness, said Barbara, and it "often leads to greater opportunities for sharing Christ. Exercising diligence in my secular work was really blessed by God. He opened some surprising opportunities for witness as a result."

Ken agreed, "I believe competence in one's field is essential to an effective ministry. Overseas as well as here at home, your knowledge of your profession and your ability on the job becomes known. If you want to command respect it is important to do your job well and to be perceived as competent by others."

"Be expert or at least very competent at your tentmaking work," George said. "The more competent you are, the easier and more credible your witness among educated people."

"There is no place in the tentmaking ministry for second best in the work you are skilled to do," Stan warned. "Being skilled in spiritual ministry and mediocre in job performance is simply not acceptable.

"I knew several who did not have a high commitment to professionalism. They thought their jobs were merely a way to get in so that they could get on with their 'real business' of being witnesses for Christ, yet their Christian witness was poor because of their inadequate, incompetent work. Incompetence on the job and strong witness for Christ are incompatible."

Commitment to Excellence
Frank had a background in civil engineering and agriculture. With some modest outside funding, he went as a tentmaker to a poor village in Thailand. A church was already there, but it was small and struggling for survival. The members of the

church were living on a bare subsistence level, so they could not support a pastor. Young men would come in and serve as pastor as long as they could earn enough through outside jobs, but as soon as they'd start a family, they'd have to move along, and the church would have to look for another young man to serve. Their pastors never lasted more than five years.

The church also had a burden to preach the Gospel to some animistic tribes further north, but they had no way of supporting missionaries.

Frank figured he could help. Under his guidance, the members of the church dammed a small stream to create an acre-sized lake. They lined the lake with plastic so that it would hold water through the dry season. Over the lake, they built chicken pens, and immediately around the lake they built pig pens. Surrounding the pig pens, they planted corn.

The idea was to feed pigs and chickens on the corn, and feed fish on the droppings from the pigs and chickens. The fish meal from the fish plus the unused parts of the pigs and chickens would then be used to fertilize the corn, and a full food cycle would be maintained, providing the villagers not only with a better diet but, hopefully, merchandise to sell—and thus an improved economy.

The operation worked so well that within four years they were selling surpluses in every area—corn, pigs, chickens, eggs, and fish. The church considered this a sacred trust. Now they could buy shoes and simple necessities, but the bulk of the money went to support a full-time pastor and to send 20 couples as missionaries to the tribal people to the north.

People who saw the operation were impressed. Some of the church members went out and planted other churches, and began similar corn/pig/chicken/fish farming programs. A whole new spirit of enthusiasm was generated as the Christians had an opportunity to share what God was doing in their midst. And their words struck home, as people were able to apply these things to their own desperate need.

Frank, having met the the deep-felt needs of the people, was able to minister the gospel effectively. The direct witness was not always his, but the success of the total venture gave impetus to the spread of the gospel. Incidentally, Frank is still in Thailand; having the greatest success of his life in sharing his faith. And that is a perfectly natural thing; his professional abilities have earned him the right to be heard.

Bill, an electrical engineer working in Asia said, "Expertise in your field helps you find and keep a job that will provide a platform for ministry. By doing a quality job, you earn the respect of your colleagues, and that helps win a hearing for the gospel and earns you more flexibility in your schedule (or a higher salary!)."

The Employment Passport
Randy and Bob had a small electronics manufacturing firm in Florida. They were burdened for Israel. They did some research to find a town in which there was no Christian witness or presence. When they found their spot, they set up shop and hired Israeli workers. They manufactured TV an-

tennas, and sold most of them outside the country.
It became a thriving little company with about 30
employees, all Israeli except Randy and Bob. From
the start, Randy and Bob made it clear that they
were Christians; they held chapel services each day.

It took time before word leaked out, but soon
some Jewish fundamentalists complained to the
mayor of the town that Randy and Bob were Christians and were proselytizing their people.

"Sorry," the mayor replied, "I cannot touch them.
These men have provided employment for our
people and have produced a positive balance of
trade. They have conducted themselves with moral
integrity. Leave them alone."

As far as the mayor was concerned, Randy and
Bob's professional competence earned them the
right to be in his community and to stay there. As
far as their employees were concerned, their competence earned them the right to be heard. Over a
period of time, many of the workers and their fami-
lies became Christians.

Randy and Bob have since turned over the operation of that business to those workers who had
proven themselves not only in their business sense
but in their Christian commitment as well. Now
they have gone to another village, remote from the
first and equally non-Christian, and started over
again.

There is no doubt that some jobs provide more
leeway in ministry, and there is nothing wrong
with seeking such positions, but among our survey
respondents, those who were successful had
worked through this issue and had come to the realization that much of any frustration they felt

about time use was the result of making a false distinction between job and ministry. It took an average of about two years for them to become aware of how to integrate work and ministry. Many tentmakers were not in their cross-cultural assignments that long.

But the point is this: whether you are planning to go for nine months, two years, or a decade, one of the most important lessons you need to learn before going overseas is that it isn't job *vs* ministry, but'job *is* ministry.

Questions for Study and Discussion

1. In your own words, summarize the message of this chapter.

2. According to the author, how can secular employment actually improve a person's ability to minister?

3. Is there anything intrinsic to any job you may consider taking that could make it hinder your ability to minister? If so,

a. What is it?

b. Can it be surmounted? If so, how? If not, is it legitimate for you to take that job anywhere— here at home *or* overseas?

4. Can you think of some illustrations of how you have effectively integrated work and ministry?

74

Have there been times when your job performance has hindered your ministry? Make a list of three ways you can improve your job performance right now so you will be a better witness.

I knew several who did not have a high commitment to professionalism. They thought their jobs were merely a way to get in so that they could get on with their "real business" of being witnesses for Christ, yet their Christian witness was poor because of their inadequate, incompetent work. Incompetence on the job and strong witness for Christ are incompatible.

CHAPTER SEVEN

You Need Professional Qualifications

J ohn Patterson, a robust 25-year old, walked into Overseas Counseling Service one day. "I think God wants me to go overseas," he said, "but I'm only a farmer . . . . "

"Yes . . . ? So what's the problem?"

"Well, what can a farmer do? I mean, I've got—what?—15 years or more of experience, I grew up on a farm. And I got my degree in animal husbandry, but . . . ."

"That's great!" we responded.

He was shocked. "What can I do with farming?"

"Oh!" we replied, "there are all kinds of opportunities! Food production is a major problem in countries around the world."

Patty came in with a desire to serve as a family counselor in Africa. She had a Ph.D. and five years' experience in family counseling.

"Yes . . . ?" we said. "And what else?"

"'What else'!" she cried. "What else do you expect? You're not going to get someone more qualified than I am!"

"For family counseling in the United States, perhaps you're right," we responded. "But family counseling is so culture-bound your North Ameri-

can training may not qualify you to counsel anywhere else except North America, among middle-
class whites. But, just for the sake of discussion,
what good will your family counseling background
be if you have to deal with a man who has eight
wives?"

Patty was crestfallen.

"Do you have any other qualifications, any other
areas of expertise?" we asked. Happily, she did, and
she was willing and able to use them for gospel witness in a closed country.

Getting in the Door

Host governments grant tentmakers the right to
enter their borders, the right to be there, on the basis of professional credentials, on expertise they feel
their country needs and cannot provide for itself
from within. It is this need for outside help that
opens the door for tentmakers. As far as many governments are concerned, "missionary" is not a skill
of critical importance to national development, but
teaching, engineering, medicine, and business man-
agement, well, that's another story!

What's Required

From the perspective of a host government, the
ideal "foreign expert" has a Ph.D., 10 to 15 years of
work experience in his field of expertise, and a willingness to work for subsistence income. Described
in that fashion, of course, there aren't too many
people who fit the bill. Happily, most governments
are willing to compromise a bit.

Opportunities—sometimes very limited—are
available for persons with almost any education or

experience. If you have quality credentials in a field, you can be virtually assured there is *some* opening for you somewhere.

As Ruth Siemens of Global Opportunities is fond of saying, "You only need one job opportunity—the right one." She mentions some of the more unusual openings she has found—everything from bee keeping to scuba diving.

The fact is, however, some fields have more opportunities than others, and if you are still in the mode of acquiring credentials, it pays to look where the opportunities are. In the following fields, there is high demand on an on-going basis.

TESOL

Those qualified to teach any basic subjects are in great demand. One subject of particular importance, however, is TESOL (*Teaching English to Speakers of Other Languages*). Increasingly, English is the *lingua franca* of the world. Governments know, if they are to have success in world markets, they need people who can speak English. This has led to a great demand for English teachers around the world, especially in Third World countries.

When I was in Bangkok, Thailand, not long ago, I spoke to an English professor. He was a native Thai. He apologized about his English pronunciation, saying it was pretty bad. It wasn't just bad—it was awful! In the area of sentence structure, grammar, and other technical aspects of the language, he was an expert. He would have put any American to shame. But in terms of pronunciation, he had a long way to go. Still, there he was teaching English to Thai young people. There is a special incentive to learn English from a native English speaker!

Being a native English speaker, however, is not enough; special training is required. Still, native English speakers can acquire TESOL skills rather easily, and the opportunities for TESOL teachers are tremendous. There are currently at least 70 countries begging for help in teaching English.

Farming

Farming is a highly marketable skill in many parts of the world. The world is hungry, and whatever can be done to help increase the food supply is most welcome.

Medicine

A lot of people with medical skills, especially those in paramedical areas, tend to downplay their expertise, but the world is sick. Medical, nursing, dental, and paramedical skills are badly needed.

Engineering, Technology, Sciences

Some of the greatest opportunities are in"high-tech" and scientific fields. In a study of opportunities available during one month recently, 3300 jobs were available. Thirteen areas represented almost 75 percent of the jobs:

Electrical Engineering — 305
Business — 297
Biological Sciences — 266
Economics/Finance — 216
Literature/Linguistics — 216
Medicine — 182
Secondary School Education — 160
Industrial Engineering — 147

Data Processing — 145
TESOL — 126
Elementary School Education — 115
Civil Engineering — 114
Air Transportation — 114

The remainder were divided among nearly 100 different work areas.

Experience

In certain subjects, a recent Ph.D. with no experience may qualify you as an expert. Even a bachelor's degree is acceptable in a few fields. But the ideal is a quality degree and several years of practical experience.

To get into a country, plan on two years' experience, minimum. As Harold, a 50-year old research chemist, said, however, "You should work in the States long enough that you will have made the adjustments necessary merely to be able to work and minister effectively in the working world. If you go overseas too soon, the difficulties of adjusting to life and ministry in the new country will simply be compounded by the difficulties of adjusting to the working world. Better to get one set of adjustments under one's belt at a time!"

Paul put it a bit differently: "You need to have your professional life under control as much as possible so God can direct you in service. What is not learned by experience and training in your own culture will not automatically be learned in another. Usually it is more difficult, not easier, to do ministry overseas. Experience in your field at home before you go is vital. A foreign country is no place to test your abilities. Whatever ministry and talents you have developed here are the ones you will be most effective in using there."

Education
Eighty-nine percent of all tentmakers we queried had at least a bachelor's degree, 35 percent had a master's, 14 percent had a doctorate, and 10 percent had post-doctoral training.

Questions for Study and Discussion

1. What professional credentials do you think you still need to acquire before going overseas? Talk it over with counselors at Tentmakers International (206-546-7555) or Global Opportunities (818-797-3233).

2. While you're working on your professional credentials, how are you doing in the other areas we've listed?

Spiritual Preparation
1) Developing your personal relationship with God.
    a. Time in the Word.
    b. Prayer.
2) Gaining ministry skills.
    a. Biblical knowledge.
    b. Experience.
        i. Cross-cultural ministry.
        ii. Leading an evangelistic Bible study.
        iii. Spiritual warfare.

Social Preparation

1) Establishing a team
   a. At home (church).
   b. To go with you.

2) Getting to know your own values.

3) Practicing and gaining skill in learning another culture/language.

Professional Preparation

1) Integrating job and ministry.

2) Gaining professional credentials.

A PERSON GOING OVERSEAS
SHOULD NOT COUNT ON HAVING
THE TIME TO REMEDY DEFICIENCIES
AFTER GETTING TO THE FIELD.
THEY SHOULD DO THEIR PREPARATION
BEFORE LEAVING THE U.S.

HEROLD

CHAPTER EIGHT

Accepting the Challenge

What's the consensus of tentmakers? Tentmaking is not for everyone. Certainly, it is no easy alternative to being a conventional missionary. Being a successful tentmaker is one of the hardest jobs ever, but the rewards that come from being used by God to help others know him is worth all the effort, pain, and frustration.

You still want to be a tentmaker? Yes? Good for you! But why? Is it because you want travel, adventure, higher pay? Forget those! Is it because you want to spread the gospel of Christ where he is not known, because you want to be obedient to your Lord and you accept the mandate of the Great Commission? You're on the right track.

First, then, settle in your mind why you want to be a tentmaker. Then diligently pursue an understanding of God's will in the matter. Remember, it's hard work, but it's an extremely satisfying way to further the kingdom of God. When you get fainthearted as you prepare for your tentmaking, remember what Paul said: "I consider that our present sufferings are not worth comparing with the glory that will be revealed in us" (Romans 8:18).

And when you are in the midst of your tentmaking, and the obstacles seem insurmountable, take note of his further declaration: "No, in all these things we are more than conquerors through him who loved us. For I am convinced that neither death nor life, neither angels nor demons, neither the present nor the future, nor any powers, neither height nor depth, nor anything else in all creation, will be able to separate us from the love of God that is in Christ Jesus our Lord" (vv. 37-39).

Tentmaking can be a wonderful way of sharing the gospel naturally, positively, and with the respect and trust of the people you work with. Tentmaking is not what we usually think of when we think of missions, but it is a very important kind of missionary endeavor, and it is the only form of missions permitted in many areas, cultures, and countries.

Be Prepared.

Accept the challenge and prepare yourself adequately for your new career. We have outlined the essential steps necessary for proper preparation. Go over them again. Commit yourself to an orderly, self-disciplined plan of fulfilling your preparation as a tentmaker. Taken one step at a time, the job won't seem nearly so intimidating.

Get a strong support group for prayer and encouragement, and go for God's best in your life. Far and away, the best support group is your own local church. Get involved there, and become submissive and accountable to them. With the help of your group, confirm in your own mind and heart that God wants you to be a tentmaker. There's

nothing wrong with admitting that your first enthusiasm had no roots in God's will, that God actually has other plans for you. You don't have to be a
tentmaker to serve God. If he wants you someplace
else, don't go against his will—you'll end up as a
poor tentmaker, a poor Christian, and a lonely indi-
vidual.

If you are still convinced, and you have your support group's agreement that you should be a tentmaker, then begin preparing yourself spiritually,
physically, mentally, and emotionally. Take to
heart the comments and advice of the veteran tentmakers who share in this book.

Spiritual Preparation

Home support.
Using your support group as a base, find a group
of Christians who will pledge to support you in the
field with prayer, letters, and encouragement in the
faith. Again, your home church is the best support
group for all these functions. Find someone to
whom you are accountable for your spiritual life.
(Once you get to the field, find a Christian there you
can count on to be honest with you and keep you in
God's will, too.) Use these other Christians as part
of God's way to maintain your spiritual health.

Learn the Bible.
Become a student of the Word. Try to schedule
at least a year of Bible school in your plans. It won't
be wasted. Study the Word on your own, and in
group Bible studies. You can't get too much of
God's Word. Become immersed in it and let it in-

fuse every aspect of your life.

Learn to Pray.

Begin (if you haven't already) to pray regularly each day. Don't just read a devotional; talk earnestly and openly with the Lord. Don't just talk to the Lord; feed yourself from the Word and with the prayerful thoughts of others through good devotionals. Don't just pray; listen for God's answers. Don't just ask; give God thanks, even in advance, before you have the answers.

Don't forget to pray for the Holy Spirit's protection from spiritual wickedness as well as life's ordinary problems. And be consistent. Pray every day, even—or especially—when you don't feel like it. Prayer is not the response of your emotions, but of your spirit to your Lord and Savior. You can't afford to miss it! Become a real prayer warrior in intercession for others.

Learn Evangelism.

Have you ever shared the gospel openly with someone? Do it now or you're unlikely to succeed in another culture. Have you ever prayed with someone to become a Christian? Learn how now so that your efforts in the field will be practiced, natural, and bring honor to the Lord rather than to your own ego.

Learn Discipleship.

The tentmakers we surveyed almost unanimously stressed the importance of being experienced at leading a discipleship group or home Bible study. This presupposes that you have been discipled by someone yourself, and have gained experience in

teaching and discipling others. Once you get someone on the field to accept Christ, what are you going
to do with him? Odds are he or she is going to be
under intense pressure and persecution for chang-
ing allegiance to Christianity. How will you handle
it? Learn now, through experience in your own culture, where the going is not so rough and you can
afford a few mistakes on the road to experience.

Cultural Preparation

Learn the Language.

Become committed to learning the local language, wherever God sends you. The tentmakers
we surveyed discovered, some from rough, first-
hand experience, that knowing the host culture's
language is always necessary for successful evangelism. Not only is communication facilitated when
you can speak the host language (you can talk to
their hearts, not just their heads), but you are also
showing respect for them and for their heritage.

Don't bring Americanism as your gospel. Bring
the true gospel, accessible to all in any language.
Don't worry about some mistakes. You will man-
age to become much more proficient once you are
in the field, and even your mistakes can be opportunities for friendly conversation with those whose
language you are trying to learn.

Learn the Culture.

Do you really believe the verse that says, "there is
neither Jew nor Greek, slave nor free, male nor fe-
male, for you are all one in Christ Jesus" (Galatians
3:28)? Then you understand the importance of

learning about the culture into which you will be thrust with your new job. To a large extent, your knowledge of and respect for the host culture reflects your knowledge of and respect for the people you encounter. If you care enough about them to share the gospel, care enough to share it in a way that earns you their respect and trust.

Professional Preparation

The third area of vital preparation for a successful tentmaker is, not surprisingly, his area of secular training. Be the best tentmaker (engineer, language teacher, draftsman, printer, etc.) you can be. All of our tentmakers found very quickly that their credibility as Christians was tightly bound to their credibility as tentmakers. It doesn't say much for the excellence of your faith if your job performance is mediocre. Also, the more expert you become in your field the more options you have.

Learn How to Integrate Your Work and Your Ministry.

Right here at home is the best place to learn that all your life is ministry. Your working hours, your breaks, your lunchtimes, your evenings, your weekends are all part of your ministry. Being a Christian involves 100 percent of your time. You really need to work on this here, or you will suffer frustration on the field because you don't have time to do "missionary" work.

Take to heart the admonition of God's Word: "One thing I do: forgetting what is behind and straining toward what is ahead, I press on toward the goal to win the prize for which God has called me heavenward in Christ Jesus" (Philippians 3:13,14).

If you try to slide by in your profession with the thought that you're doing God a favor by serving as a tentmaker, your co-workers will find you out and lose respect for the Lord at the same time they lose respect for you.

Peter warned, "Keep a clear conscience, so that those who speak maliciously against your good behavior in Christ may be ashamed of their slander. It is better, if it is God's will, to suffer for doing good than for doing evil" (1 Peter 3:16,17).

Become Involved Here.

Wherever you are going to serve as a tentmaker you will need cross-cultural experience. Get involved now in inner-city work. Work with international students. Experience as a short-term missionary gives good cross-cultural exposure. Peace Corps is a valid opportunity of getting some cross-cultural experience. Be on the lookout for immigrants in your area. They are all over, and many are from the most unreached areas of the world.

Read Some Good Books.

To get started, I highly recommend these four. There are many others on each aspect of preparation, but these are key:

On the Crest of the Wave by C. Peter Wagner. This is an easily-read introduction to current missions. What God is doing and how we can become involved.

In the Gap by David Bryant. Introduces the concept of being a "World Christian."

Today's Tentmaker by J. Christy Wilson. A classic on the concept of tentmaking.

God's New Envoys by Ted Yamamori. A recent volume especially concerned with relief and development opportunities, but with much valuable information pertaining to tentmaking in general.

Serving God

As a tentmaker, you have the rare privilege of being on the front lines of God's war against sin, of being in the vanguard of Christian missions today. Be proud to be a tentmaker. Rejoice that God has chosen you to be a part of fulfilling the Great Commission: "Therefore go and make disciples of all nations, . . . teaching them to obey everything I have commanded you. And surely I will be with you always, to the very end of the age" (Matthew 28:19).

So you want to be a tentmaker? Be a good one!

The Hamilton Tentmaker Survey: Summary of Report #1

A questionnaire with 132 items was sent to over 800 people who are serving or have served overseas in a tentmaking capacity. The names were obtained from over 100 sources. Study findings are based on 406 survey responses.

A system was developed and tested to measure the elusive quality of effectiveness. 30 parameters were chosen and quantified. When applied to the respondents of the survey, a normal distribution curve resulted. The backgrounds of those in the upper 16 percent (those rated very good to excellent) were analyzed in depth.

The study revealed that highly-rated tentmakers had the following characteristics:

• *They had led an evangelistic Bible study before going overseas.*

It is felt that this is significant because conventional witnessing methods, such as door-to-door visitation, passing out tracts, holding street meetings, etc., are not wise or even possible in many places where tentmakers work. Building relationships and earning the right to be heard are key. An evangelistic Bible study is a fine strategy.

• *Their main reason for going was to share the Gospel of Christ.*

Travel, money, or a desire to be independent were not strong motivating factors. Without motivation to share the Gospel, less effective tentmakers quickly burn out in the often hostile environments.

• *They believe God called them to be tentmakers.*

When the going got tough, many indicated it was their deep conviction of God's calling that carried them through. The emphasis was on absolute assurance that this is where God wanted them.

• *They had experience in actively sharing their faith at home.*

Compared to the "average" tentmaker, twice as many of these highly-effective tentmakers witnessed about Christ overseas, and three times as many led others to Christ.

• *They had strong relationships with their local home church.*

Their attendance and participation was consistent, and their churches considered their tentmaking work to be a true mission activity. Most were commissioned by, reported back to, and felt accountable to their churches.

• *They recruited others to be tentmakers.*

They realized that if the Gospel is to be shared with the two-thirds of the world that has never heard the name of Jesus, tentmakers must go.

A modified Engel scale helped evaluate effectiveness. The six questions moved progressively from leading people with no knowledge of Christianity:

a. to a knowledge of such;
b. to an understanding of the fundamentals of the Gospel;
c. to a recognition of personal need;
d. to conversion;
e. to incorporation into a fellowship of Christians; and
f. to an active propagator of the faith.

It was on this scale that the very effective tentmakers really separated themselves from average Christians overseas.

For further informaton on the survey, or for a copy of the full report ($10), write to Don Hamilton, TMQ Research, 312 Melcanyon Road, Duarte, CA 91010. (818) 303-5533.

Continued from front flap

skills as the window through which your Christian commitment can shine.

Engineers, language teachers, computer specialists, and agricultural workers are just a few of the kinds of Christians needed. Tentmaking is an exciting addition to professional missionary work. It is also demanding and requires rigorous training and Christian maturity.

So you want to be a tentmaker? Be a good one!

DON HAMILTON is a former executive with the Xerox Corporation, founder of the Association of Church Missions Committees (ACMC), and former Executive Director of Overseas Counseling Service.

He is currently Director of TMQ Research, dedicated to facilitating tentmaker training and growth. TMQ Research is actively engaged in identifying the factors for successful tentmaking. These include the areas of education, training, background, experience, ministry, personality, and commitment.

Don Hamilton's pioneering research on tentmaking, some of which forms the basis of **Tentmakers Speak**, was described by Dr. Dean Kliewer, Director of Research Ministries for Link-Care Center, as a "landmark" study.